A FUN BOOK OF TOUCH

FEEL!

This edition published 1992
by BCA by arrangement with
WAYLAND (PUBLISHERS) LTD

CN 5571

First published in 1990 by
Firefly Books Limited
61 Western Road, Hove
East Sussex BN3 1JD, England

© Copyright 1990 Firefly Books Limited

© Copyright Neil Morris (text) Peter Stevenson (artwork)

Editor: Francesca Motisi

Typeset by DP Press Limited, Sevenoaks, Kent
Printed and bound in Belgium by Casterman S.A.

A FUN BOOK OF TOUCH

FEEL!

Written by Neil Morris
Illustrated by Peter Stevenson

BCA

LONDON · NEW YORK · SYDNEY · TORONTO

Mary is having a birthday party.
After tea Mum says.
    'I've made up a special game.'
The children ask what's in the big bag.
    'You have to feel and tell me, that's the game!' Mary's mum says.

6

'Can I do the music?' 'I want to look in the bag!' 'Me first!' shout the children. Everyone passes the bag around. When the music stops, the person holding the bag puts their hand in and tells the others what they can feel. Everyone has a guess at what it is!

8

It's Lisa's turn first.
'I can feel something prickly,' she says. 'But it's smooth on one side.'

When the music stops again, Mary
is holding the bag.
  'The thing I'm feeling is soft and
very squashy,' she says.

'It felt horrible!' Tim tells his friends. 'Wet and slimy!'

'Shhhhh,' Kelly says, 'I'm trying to listen.'

'That's cheating,' says Mary.

'No, it isn't,' Kelly says, 'because I can feel little things round a ring. I just want to hear if they make a noise.'

Max can't wait to have his go.

'I'm stroking something soft and cuddly and furry. It's got long ears and a fluffy tail. Can anyone guess what it is?'

18

'Can I take mine home?' Emma asks.
'It's got four corners and opens up.
I think it's made of paper.'

'Sticky, very sticky!' Peter says.
'With little bumps on top.'

Lucy can feel something smooth and hard with a handle.

'Whatever it is,' she says, 'it's open at the top and closed at the bottom.'

'Stop tickling, you silly thing!'
Barry giggles. 'It's very light and feathery.'

'I'm warming my hands on it,' Ann tells the others. 'When I poke it, something moves inside. It's rubbery.'

There's just one more thing left in the bag.
Dan tries to squeeze it, but it's too hard.
He counts four round shapes that
spin around.

'It must be something with wheels,'
he says.

Here are the objects the children
felt in the bag.
Did you guess right?

Discussion points

FEEL explores the sense of touch. In the story the children are playing a game of 'Feelies' and the reader can join in and have a guess, according to the description and the pictures. Talk about the objects and what they feel like. Use words like hard, soft, smooth, silky, squashy, prickly, coarse, rough, wet, dry, furry, etc. After reading the story, you could have your own game of 'Feelies'.

4/5 +   What games do you play when it's
6/7   your birthday party? Have you ever played 'Feelies'? It's a touching game. Can you spot the extra guest? (It's Mary's pet mouse!)

9   What's prickliest in the picture? Can you think of some other prickly things? (cactus, holly, rose) Now touch something smooth.

11   You can shape squashy things with your hands. What's your favourite squashy food? Marshmallows? What happens when you squeeze a squashy tomato?

12/13   Tim doesn't like wet and slimy things. Some wet things are nice, but most slimy things aren't. Hold an ice cube in your hand – what happens? It'll either slip out or melt.

15   All these round things feel hard. Which one do you think is making a noise?

16/17   Mouse feels soft too. But who feels furriest? Do you like stroking cuddly pets?

19   Paper feels smooth. When you crunch it up, it crackles. Some paper is rough (sandpaper). Do you like comics?

21   Sticky things often taste sweet, because sugar is sticky. Can you think of some more sticky things? (lollipop, plasters, glue, etc.) Not all sticky things are for eating! Don't forget to wash your hands after touching something sticky!

22   Mouse is cheating – he is having a look instead of a feel!

25   What happens when you get tickled? Some people are much more ticklish than others.

27   You can feel warmth with your hands, but you can also feel it with your feet. You could use your feet to feel all these things. Are your feet as good as your hands for finding out what they are touching?

28/29   Hard things can't be squeezed. But you don't need wheels to spin around. Mouse is spinning around by its tail.

30/31   Look back through the book and compare each description with the objects the children found in the bag. How would you have described these things? Find some of them in your home; touch them and think about the way they feel. Make up a bag of objects that feel different, and test yourself or a friend.